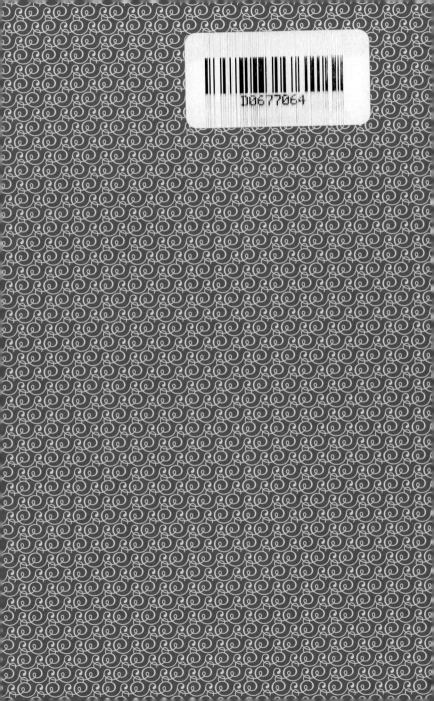

The Love Magic Book

Also in this series:

The Good Spell Book
Love Charms, Magical Cures,
and Other Practical Sorcery

The Fortune-Telling Book
Reading Crystal Balls, Tea Leaves,
Playing Cards, and Everyday
Omens of Love and Luck

The Dream Book
Dream Spells, Nighttime Potions
and Rituals, and Other
Magical Sleep Formulas

The Love Spell Box
A Pack of 30 Love Cards and
a Book of Spells to Enhance
Your Love Life

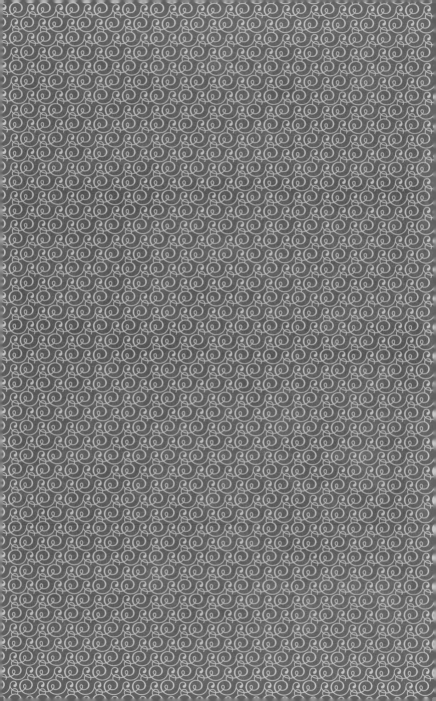

The love magic book

by Gillian Kemp

POTIONS
FOR PASSION
and
RECIPES
FOR ROMANCE

Little, Brown and Company

Boston New York London

To my honorary and honorable
    advisor, Ian McCorquodale,
and his wife, Bryony,
    Katie Boyle and her husband,
        Sir Peter Saunders,
David and Sylvia,
            to the one I love,
and to you, the reader.
Also to my Yorkshire terrier,
        Rosie Posy.

Contents

Caraway seeds sprinkled
in your lover's pockets are
believed to keep the flame
of your life faithful to you.

*L*ove magic is the most potent and ancient of all magic, an eternal light that has existed since time immemorial and lives in every person. We all possess love magic as our natural source of life. It is the power that keeps us alive when we feel like dying and the power that makes us feel like dying when a lover's affections for us fade. Love magic makes the world go round as an energy that transcends Earth, space, and time. Since it is the strongest and most accessible of all magic, we can easily woo love our way by tapping into this love life source. ¶ Two people in love exude a physical glow, a flowing and electrical energy visible to others. This love light is just as much within you as it is in all that you see, hear, smell, touch, and taste. Love magic doubles every power you possess; linking to this power is like putting a plug into an electrical socket. By connecting to this source, you can establish a love link with every living part of nature; love light will enter your life eternally. In aligning yourself with this frequency, you can harness the living power of love and easily influence romance. Supernatural forces ruled by love will then become sympathetic to your inner resonance and will obey the laws of nature you invoke through magic to accelerate the natural process of life. By treading the mystical pathway, you will find the love you seek. ¶ Such love magic has been at work since the mythical days of Cupid, whose arrows still pierce the hearts of the lovelorn. Throughout history, Cupid's arrows have found their mark with legendary lovers such as Cleopatra and Mark Antony, and Romeo and Juliet. ¶ You can sense love magic in the magnetic thrill you feel when someone attracts you. Time stands still and all else pales as the flame of passion is ignited and a chain reaction begins. Love magic spells work by enhancing the link between you and the one you desire by calling on the assistance of influential divine powers. ¶ Love acts as a catalyst to make your wishes materialize. Your inner thoughts send magnetic vibrations into the ether, or energy, creating waves that extend outside yourself. When you feel someone's glance, you are sensing the etheric waves from that person. The ether has tides like the sea, with waves of increasing strength that determine what will happen. You can either harmonize or conflict with these forces of change. Since the ether is influenced by your thoughts, it is a subtler plane of energy than matter and can be permeated by words. ¶ Spells are words of power that control the driving impulse in the ether, the invisible energy behind things that can be seen. Magic is simply concentrating and directing your focused thoughts to any aim or person to achieve a desired result. Knowing your own heart is most important. The rest is as simple as aiming a ball at a net or a dart at a dartboard. The spells that follow will help you aim Cupid's arrow to find your own true love. You can also reverse the power of spells if you have a change of heart. All this and more await you in these magical pages.

Attracting
LOVE

It is natural to love another person. Love is both ecstatic happiness and deep despair, both sweet and bitter. Your mind may advise you not to love a worthless or unfaithful person, but the heart will continue to love because it cannot accept reason. When wishing for a new relationship, be wise. When you first fall in love, you see a fantasy of the person because you do not know the real him or her. You imagine that you know this person, but you don't see the flaws, because only his or her best side is being shown to you. Remember that in each relationship you risk losing your heart to love. Here are spells and potions to attract your heart's desire.

[15]

To meet your intended

Place two pink candles in candleholders and arrange them next to each other, a foot apart. One candle represents you and the other symbolizes your sweetheart. Tie a knot of red ribbon, cord, or string loosely around the candleholders. ¶ On the next day, untie the ribbon, move the candleholders closer, and tie them together again. Light both candles and let them burn for a while, then snuff them out. Do this for three, five, seven, or nine days until the candleholders are touching on the last day. Sit with the candles while they burn on the final day, then snuff them out. Untie the ribbon and keep it among your personal possessions for protection as a love amulet.

To aim and fire
cupid's arrow

Take a red candle, as red represents life and passion.
The light in the flame symbolizes the good power in
a person. With a pin, inscribe the name of the one
you love around the top of the candle. Pierce the
inscription with a new pin, pressing it through the
wick so the pin tip emerges on the opposite side of
the candle. As you press the pin into the wax, say:
*"Through your name to the wick, I aim for your heart with this can-
dle I prick."* Place the candle in a holder and position
the pin tip so that it faces the direction in which your
lover lives. Light the candle and sit with it while sending love to your desired. When the flame has burned
through the name and pin, snuff out the candle.
The candle can be relit at another time, but should
be buried with the pin once it is too small to light.

Carry anise and love will
follow. Another way to
attract a new love is to write
the name of your intended in
red ink on a bay leaf and
wear the leaf in your shoe.

To attract
a new romance

Cast this spell on a night when the new moon is a crescent in the sky. Place a pink rose and a red rose in a narrow-stemmed vase. At a few minutes before midnight, sprinkle three drops of rose oil into the vase's water. Within fourteen days, a new person will enter your life. If you like this person, place the roses in a clean, white envelope. Sleep with the envelope under your pillow and speak the name of your intended three times before going to sleep. You will draw your desired to you.

[17]

To beckon
a heart to yours

On a Friday night, write your intended's name in red ink on nine small pieces of red paper to ignite passion. Wrap a pinch of dried mint in each piece of paper or smear each piece with mint oil. ¶ Throw one of the packets into a hearth or bonfire and speak your lover's name repeatedly until the packet has burned away. Do the same with the remaining eight sachets, and as each one burns, your love will grow closer.

Bay, ruled by the sun, will bring sunshine into the places you go and the people you meet.

To receive
a telephone call
or e-mail

Take a whole nutmeg and wrap it in a red ribbon while saying: "[*Name of person*], *you will contact me.*" Light a white candle for purity and place the wrapped nutmeg in front of the candle as it burns for an hour. The nutmeg represents your lover's brain; the ribbon represents your desires. The ribbon will transfer your wish to the one you long for and will prompt him or her to get in touch with you. Snuff out the candle and keep the nutmeg in its wrapping by your telephone or computer. The one you desire should call or e-mail within seven days. ¶ To encourage more contact, write your love interest's name in cursive writing in a semicircular shape, using green ink on blue paper. Join your own name with the name of the one you desire, continuing the semicircle until it is a complete circle. Repeat the writing seven times on top of the original lettering. Sprinkle a few drops of lavender oil onto the paper and rub the oil over the paper. (Mercury, the planet that governs communication, also rules lavender.) Place the piece of paper under your computer or telephone. As the scent fades, rub more lavender oil onto the piece of paper bearing your names to continue the contact with your desired one.

Love
at your door

To draw your sweetheart to visit your home, write his or her name on a small piece of paper on the night of a new moon. Fold the piece of paper in half to conceal the name, and write your name on the outside. Fold the paper in half again and sprinkle the outside with three drops of rose oil to attract love. ¶ Place the piece of paper under the doormat. The one you desire is likely to arrive within the twenty-eight-day moon cycle, just before a full moon. Do not let impatience deter you from keeping the piece of paper in place.

[19]

To receive a visit
or invitation

Cloves are a love attraction. Take a small orange and a lemon, and stud both with cloves. The orange represents your lover and the lemon symbolizes you. Whenever you wish for a visit or an invitation to your lover's home, place the orange and lemon side by side on a windowsill or in a corner of your home that points in the direction of his or her house. If a relationship ends amicably, bury the orange or lemon side by side. If you wish to break the spell and sever communication either temporarily or permanently, bury them apart.

To beckon love

At sunrise or on rising, anoint a red candle with rose oil. With your fingertips, stroke the oil from the top of the candle—representing the North Pole—down to the center. Then stroke the oil upward from the base—representing the South Pole—up to the center. Light the candle and let it burn for an hour. Relight the candle daily until it has melted away in your presence on the last day. Like sunshine, love will arrive in your life.

Two halves
make a whole

[20]

Cut a coconut in half, leaving milk in both halves. Place a floating candle in both shells—one candle to represent you and the other to symbolize the one you love. If you need more liquid, fill the shells with water. Let the candles burn until they extinguish naturally. Your other half will sail in soon.

Infuse nine violet flowers in about a quarter of a cup of boiling water. When the infusion is cold, pour it into a vial or a small, clean pill bottle. A little of the concoction dabbed on your lips will

To attract
loving desire

On a Friday night, take a rose and trim the stem to about one inch long. Pierce the stem with a pin so that the pin tip emerges on the opposite side. Fill a screw-top jar with water and drop the rose in. ¶ For seven consecutive nights, light a pink candle and place the jar containing the rose beside it, snuffing out the candle just before you go to sleep. On the final night, remove the rose from the jar, place it in a dish of water, and snuff out the candle. When the rose fades, scatter the petals into the wind. Love should arrive within twenty-eight days from when you commence your spell.

[21]

To enchant your
first kiss

To enchant the one you love, wear a sprig of mint close to your heart. When you kiss for the first time, hold your lover's left hand in your left hand and make a wish. The charm of linking left hands even for one moment leads two hearts to feel and merge as one. You will know that your charm has worked if your lover's left hand moves close to his or her heart during or after kissing you

attract sweet kisser to you, because violets are ruled by the love planet, Venus.

Three wishes

To make your first wish, place two roses of any color in a vase of water and position a pink candle on either side. Light both candles and move them closer and closer toward the roses. Each time you move the burning candles closer to the roses, drop a small pinch of ground mace into the flames and speak your wish aloud. Snuff out the candles when they cannot be moved any closer to the roses. When the roses fade days later, place the blooms or petals in a piece of paper (upon which you have written the name of the one you desire). Fold the paper to contain the rose and love's essence. Keep the charm under your pillow or close to your heart, and you will keep your lover's heart close to the sentiments of yours. ¶ Make your second wish by using another pink candle. Pink is the color of romance. Leaving space at the candle base so that it can still fit into the holder, inscribe your wish lengthwise from the wick to the base, using a pin. Place the candle in the holder and light it. Close your eyes and make a love wish. Sit with the candle while it burns through the inscription, then snuff the candle out. ¶ To make your third wish, take a pebble and hold it cupped in your hands. Close your eyes, and without allowing any other thought to intrude, impart your wish from your mind into the stone. Dwell on what it is that you desire to accomplish. Place the pebble in a clean thread handkerchief or silk scarf. Later pass the stone into the hands of the one you wish to obey your command. By taking the stone, the person will subconsciously embrace the thought, and your wish will be his or her command.

Bewitching potion

Into a glass of water placed in moonlight, sprinkle a large pinch each of fennel seeds, powdered nutmeg, grated ginger, dried or fresh thyme, and dried or fresh basil. Leave the concoction to steep overnight. Strain the brew into a clean glass bottle. When dabbed on your lover's clothes, a few drops of the potion will bewitch your love.

[23]

Passion potion

Light a pink candle anointed with vervain oil and frankincense oil. Pour equal amounts of orange blossom water, rose water, and violet water into a glass perfume bottle. Replace the lid and shake the bottle in front of the flame. Hold the bottle, looking into the potion, and envision your ideal partner. Snuff the candle out. When dabbed on your pulse points, the potion will attract passion.

predicting
love's course

There are three stages of attraction: visual, vocal, and physical. When you see someone and are drawn to him or her, this visual attraction is the first stage. You can also see whether he or she responds to you in the same way. Second, when you hear the voice of the one you admire, your attraction deepens if you like what you hear. The third, physical phase develops from wanting to be close to this person that you have found emotions for. ¶ The course of true love can be predicted through divinations, bringing peace of mind and hope. It is reassuring and amusing to watch a love dilemma unfold while knowing the outcome in advance. Reserve, patience, and faith are part of the waiting game that is one of the pains of love. You can divine in solitude, as well as predict with one or more friends. ¶ Listen to your intuition as a new relationship progresses. A kiss will tell you whether or not there is love in your heart for a suitor. If you do not like kissing when kissed, your intuition is telling you that the relationship is wrong from the start. Without love in your heart, you cannot kiss when kissed.

It is said to be unlucky to look at yourself and your partner reflected as a couple in a mirror. It is an omen that you will part.

Is my lover true?

Light a candle outdoors near your lover's home. If the flame quivers in your direction, your beloved's heart dwells on you. If the flame flickers in the direction of your sweetheart's home, his or her thoughts for you are not particularly strong and may be wavering.

To meet again

Before you meet your love, light a white or silver candle on the night of a new moon. Sprinkle three drops of rose oil and three drops of clove oil onto a cotton handkerchief. Snuff out the candle. ¶ From time to time during your date, hold the handkerchief in your left hand to imbue the potion into your skin. On parting company with your loved one, touch his or her right hand with your left hand, and he or she will absorb the spiritual essence of the love potion and be driven by an irresistible desire to see you again.

[28]

A wedding when the moon is waxing — becoming full — is heaven blessed for increase of happiness and wealth. The day of a full moon is also a fruitful omen.

Armchair magic

When the one you love is not sitting with you, armchair magic is a strong force in drawing the one you desire to you. In the comfort of your own home, sit in an armchair and hold an item related to your love, such as an article of clothing, a signature, or something else personal. A photograph is a very strong psychic link to use for spell casting. You do not necessarily need an object belonging to him or her. Inscribing a candle with the name of the one you desire makes the candle, when lit, a miniature version of the love of your life. Say your heartfelt wish out loud into the object, candle, or your lover's mouth if you are using a photograph: *"[Name of person], you know you love me. Prove your love for me by actions, not words."* ¶ If you are using a candle, snuff it out when you are finished and take your lover's item or photograph into your bedroom. Keep it there every night, even after you have achieved your heart's desire. Remove the article from your bedroom only when you want to remove the person you named from your life.

To marry during a waning moon is the least fortuitous omen, heralding a demise of good fortune.

Garden magic

Flowers emit and receive various signals according to the personality of the planet that rules each plant. Understanding a flower's characteristic links you to that flower's energy, carrying your wish into realms beyond. If you know the birth sign of the one you love, you can establish a link with your sweetheart through the tree, flowering plant, or herb ruling your lover's zodiac sign. To make love grow, use a small rose plant in a pot, or cast your spell with a garden rose to represent you. Next to the rose, plant the flower linked to the specific zodiac sign of the one you love.

ARIES (March 21–April 19)
Garlic, ruled by Mars

TAURUS (April 20–May 20)
Heather, ruled by Venus

GEMINI (May 21–June 21)
Lily of the valley or dill, ruled by Mercury

CANCER (June 22–July 22)
Lettuce or pumpkin, ruled by the moon

LEO (July 23–August 22)
Marigolds, ruled by the sun

VIRGO (August 23–September 22)
Lavender, ruled by Mercury

LIBRA (September 23–October 23)
Thyme or strawberries, ruled by Venus

SCORPIO (October 24–November 21)
Poppies or onions, ruled by Mars

SAGITTARIUS (November 22–December 21)
Dandelion or chervil, ruled by Jupiter

CAPRICORN (December 22–January 19)
Pansies, ruled by Saturn

AQUARIUS (January 20–February 18)
Gladiolus or campion, ruled by Saturn

PISCES (February 19–March 20)
Sage, ruled by Jupiter

Flowers divination

Pick or buy twice as many flowers as you have potential lovers. Place the flowers in pairs—one flower to represent you and the other to symbolize someone you like. Write the name of each sweetheart on separate pieces of paper so that you have as many pieces of paper as budding lovers. In your bedroom, away from prying eyes, place the pairs of flowers on top of each correspondingly named piece of paper. If after ten days any two flowers in a pair entwine, it is a sign of a good love match. If one flower in a pair turns away from the other, you will reject your prospective lover or he or she will rebuff you. If a flower opens, love will bloom. If a flower dies early, so too will the affections of the person that flower represents.

Birthday flower divination

To divine the course of your love, place a flower to represent you and a flower to represent your lover in a glass vase. Use the flowers that correspond to your and your lover's birthday months.

    JANUARY: *Snowdrop or crocus*
    FEBRUARY: *Violet*
    MARCH: *Daffodil*
    APRIL: *Primrose*
    MAY: *White lily*
    JUNE: *Wild rose*
    JULY: *Carnation*
    AUGUST: *White heather*
    SEPTEMBER: *Daisy*
    OCTOBER: *Sunflower*
    NOVEMBER: *Chrysanthemum*
    DECEMBER: *Holly*

Place the vase on a windowsill or in sunlight. Days later, when the sunlight has turned the water murky, gaze into the center of the water at the base of the vase. Allow your imagination to drift. Visions of people and scenes will appear to predict what you might expect with your lover. When you are outside, watch for the first flower of the season; the day of the week you see it growing is premonitory.

🛡 **MONDAY**: *Your visions are a sign of good luck for you.*

🛡 **TUESDAY**: *Financial success will come.*

🛡 **WEDNESDAY**: *A marriage proposal and wedding will arrive sooner than you think.*

🛡 **THURSDAY**: *Hard work lies ahead.*

🛡 **FRIDAY**: *Expect a surprising gift of love.*

🛡 **SATURDAY**: *Expect a surprising gift of money.*

🛡 **SUNDAY**: *A love affair will exceed your wildest expectations.*

To bind this lover to you, tie the flowers together and press them in tissue paper for twenty-eight days, then keep them in a book.

Daisy divination

[33]

Get a bunch of daisies and put them on a table. With eyes closed, take a handful while asking how many days you will wait to be asked for a date. If you prefer you may ask in terms of weeks or months. Open your eyes and count the picked daisies. The number of flowers represents the number of days you will wait. Daisy divination can also predict how many months or years you will wait to wed.

Finding a ring on any day is an omen of romance.

Rose
divination

Take two roses, entwine each stem around the other, and tie them in place with red or pink thread. Place them in a vase with water. If any petals appear to darken in color within a day or two, your intended's love for you is growing deeper and stronger.

Rosemary
divination

[34]

Pick a sprig of rosemary while saying: *"Rosemary, rosemary, I pluck thee, tonight for my true love to see."* Sleep with the herb under your pillow to dream of your next romantic encounter.

Friends and flowers

Get a bouquet of flowers—try to include borage, rosemary, violet, geranium, mint, nettle, chive, eyebright, periwinkle, or primrose. Have each friend pick one. Fill a quarter of an ice-cube tray with water, and have each person place a flower in a cube. Top the cubes with more water to ensure the flowers do not float to the top of the cubes. Place the trays in the freezer. When the cubes are frozen, put them in a bowl of water and light a white or silver floating candle in the center while everyone makes a wish together. The person whose flower emerges from the ice and floats to the top of the water first is the person whose wish will be the first to come true. Each minute it takes for a flower to emerge is interpreted as the number of days or months in which a lovers' meeting will take place. ¶ To divine love attraction, place two flower cubes in the bowl of water around the floating silver candle. If the flowers touch when the ice melts, you and your lover will meet. Time can be determined intuitively as sooner or later, depending on how long it takes for the flowers to touch.

Dice divination

Each person should write his or her lovers' names on individual pieces of paper. A photograph of each lover can also be used. One or more dice should be cast upon each piece of paper or photograph to divine a yes or no answer. An odd number on the dice answers yes, an even number, no.

To dream of your lover, sleep with nine vanilla beans wrapped in a silk scarf or handkerchief placed under your pillow.

Playing-card divination

With your lover, shuffle a pack of fifty-two playing cards. Select thirteen cards from anywhere in the pack and lay them in a row. If both a king and a heart appear in the first line, it is a sign that you have met your match. ¶ Your partner has met his or her match if a diamond and a queen appear in the thirteen cards he or she randomly selects from a deck of fifty-two cards. If neither appears, keep shuffling and begin again. The number of times the cards are spread before they appear represents the number of lovers you will meet before your match arrives. Reshuffle the pack and choose thirteen new cards to predict how smoothly the course of true love will run. If hearts predominate, love will last. Diamonds reveal many social engagements. An ace of diamonds foretells an engagement ring. A predominance of clubs shows that common interests such as studies and hobbies will keep love alive. More spades than other cards is a sign that the relationship is likely to be fraught with difficulties and may end in tears.

It is said to be a lucky omen of a happy marriage to wed a person whose date of

Playing-card divination with friends

If friends know your wish, this can help it come true. Friends' thoughts direct Cupid's arrow to the heart of the one you love and can help you win your heart's desire. One thought multiplied by many minds is stronger than one mind alone. ¶ Gather your friends around a lit pink candle and will the flame to rise while the one in love shuffles a pack of fifty-two cards. Everyone should then keep the flame high by thinking and willing the fire to burn brightly. ¶ While the flame is narrow and high, the lovelorn who is seeking an answer must throw one pinch of salt into the flame while randomly selecting one card before the flame stops burning blue. If a heart card is chosen, love is destined to occur with the one desired. A diamond signifies great happiness. A spade signifies retreat because the desired will be detrimental to the lovelorn. A club means that difficulties and delays will not divide two hearts destined to beat as one. Words of love will be exchanged when the two eventually meet. Once the lovelorn's question has been answered, those present should blow the candle out while wishing the same wish.

birth is the same as your own
or the same date but
a different year.

Love destiny
foretold

Alone or with friends, remove the twelve cards that compose the suit of hearts. Place the queen of hearts in a central position on a table or the floor. If not alone, you and your friends should sit in a circle around the queen of hearts card. Take the king and jack from the diamond, club, and spade suits. Shuffle the kings and jacks into the hearts suit and place the seventeen cards randomly in a circle around the queen of hearts. ¶ Place a bottle on the queen card, close your eyes, and spin the bottle. When the bottle stops spinning, the card that the mouth of the bottle faces signifies a person who loves you. If the card is a king or jack of hearts or diamonds, your suitor is fair-haired and fair-complexioned. He is dark-haired and dark-complexioned if the card is a club or spade. ¶ Any numbered card the bottle is facing signifies either a time of day when a meeting will occur or the number of days, weeks, or months that will go by before a romantic rendezvous. With your eyes closed, spin the bottle again. If the mouth points to a number instead of a court card, this signifies a delay. A two of hearts on the first spin could mean two o'clock, two weeks, the second of the month, or two months' time. The second spin adds detail: the bottle facing the five of hearts will reveal five o'clock, or a meeting with two other people in five days', weeks', or months' time, or in the fifth month of the year. ¶ The first intuitive thought that comes into your mind with each spin of the bottle is a divine thought, so follow and build upon the hour, day, week, or month initially chosen by the first spin. ¶ Spin the bottle until you are satisfied and feel settled in your mind with whom and when you will date. If friends are with you, keep your place in the circle, allowing the next person to spin the bottle and prophesy his or her love destiny.

Clothing magic

The best side of your personality can be enhanced or strengthened when you wish by wearing colors that suit you. The planet that rules your date of birth may help you to know which colors enhance your personality, because clothes and accessories carry your magnetism. What you wear sends light and receives light. You may judge what you might expect from a potential lover according to how your suitor responds to the colors and clothes you choose to wear when meeting. When you try on an outfit in front of a mirror for a special event, your initial response will tell you how right or wrong that outfit is for the occasion. The person you are wearing it for will respond positively if you feel a positive response to yourself when you look in the mirror. Once you have decided on what you will wear, do not change your mind, because your instinctive light has guided you to make a choice. ¶ You can use the power of color to influ-

ence the environment around you. A person will respond instinctively on the level of the color you display. In this way you will understand whether a person's psyche is either in harmony or flowing against the tide flowing through you. By experimenting with certain outfits of color, you will find that some repeatedly bring success while others cause friction for one reason or another. ¶ Spirits are attracted by certain colors they are sympathetic to. The colors of the spectrum transmit strong magnetic vibrations where spirits link in the ether.

❧ RED ☙
*Energizing and passionate, red negates a depressed,
gloomy, or lethargic mood.*

❧ PINK ☙
The color of romance, pink attracts and emits love.

❧ ORANGE ☙
*Revitalizing, like the sun. Worn alone, it is a marriage sign
that can speed a love affair to the altar.*

❧ YELLOW ☙
*Mentally stimulating, yellow is said to encourage circulating
energies as well as have a good influence on financial gains.*

❧ GREEN ☙
*A color of fertility and also of hope because it is
the color of nature.*

❧ TURQUOISE ☙
*Being a combination of blue and green, turquoise has
a healing and brightening influence.*

⚜ BLUE ⚜

"Blue means true." It is believed to be both calming and inspirational. It is a good color to wear when quick-tempered or overanxious.

⚜ PURPLE ⚜

Purple is a color of spiritual protection, luxury, success, and social advancement into regal circles.

⚜ BLACK ⚜

Depressing when frequently worn, black can negate the wearer's personality. Of all clothes, black should be cleaned or aired more frequently because it absorbs and emits negativity.

⚜ BROWN ⚜

The color of the earth, golden brown is positive, but dark brown is grounding.

⚜ GRAY ⚜

Being the color of clouds, gray does not have a cheerful influence. It encourages negativity to linger.

⚜ WHITE ⚜

White exudes honesty, purity, and innocence. An adverse reaction to white reveals a wish to conceal light or truth.

⚜ SILVER ⚜

Associated with the moon, silver influences both calm and turbulent emotions. It can give life to dormant emotions and bring feelings to a peak of clarity.

⚜ GOLD ⚜

Gold is believed to induce happiness and to be the luckiest color to wear for a job interview because it is the color of wealth.

A dowsing pendulum

When undecided about what to wear, dowsing can resolve your dilemma because you instinctively possess the ancient art. Cave paintings in the northern Sahara dated 6000 B.C. picture cavemen dowsing for water with a forked twig. Ancient Egyptians, Chinese, and Peruvians also practiced dowsing to search for metals, fuel, and water. Instead of a rod, you may prefer to use a dowsing pendulum. One can be made simply by suspending a ring or door key from a length of thread. The strand, about eight inches long, should be wound around the forefinger of the hand you use to write with and held in place by that hand's thumb. ¶ Spread the items you are considering wearing on your bed or hang them from the backs of dining chairs. Hold the pendulum over each individual item while concentrating on the thought or asking aloud: *"Shall I wear this to* [*meet someone or to visit a location*] *?"* Decide in your mind that the pendulum will swing in a clockwise circular movement to answer yes and an anticlockwise circle to reply no. If the dowsing pendulum swings backward and forward, rephrase your question.

Divining the best lover

Write the names of potential suitors on separate pieces of paper. Hold the pendulum over each piece of paper individually while speaking these words aloud or in your head: *"Is [name of person] right for me?"* Yes is the answer if the pendulum swings in a clockwise motion, no if counterclockwise. Backward and forward motions show indecision as well as bad timing.

Love dowsing divination

Your dowsing pendulum can answer love conundrums. Ask a question aloud or silently by concentrating your mind on your question. Yes is the answer if the pendulum swings in a clockwise circle. A counterclockwise motion means no. Backward and forward swinging reveals indecision. In this case, try again later.

[43]

> *Are his/her feelings sincere?*
> *Does he/she truly love me?*
> *Should I continue this relationship?*
> *Should I forget this relationship?*
> *Will we meet?*
> *When will we meet? (Will it be in one day? one week? at the next dance?)*
> *Should I show my feelings when we meet?*
> *Should I be reserved when we meet?*
> *Will we kiss when we meet?*
> *Will he/she ask for another date?*
> *Is [name of person] faithful to me?*
> *Is he/she unfaithful with someone I know?*
> *Is he/she dating [name of person you suspect]?*

Love
Lithomancy

Lithomancy is an ancient method to predict fortunes from candlelight reflecting colors in common, precious, or semiprecious stones, or colored glass pebbles. Stones that attract your attention should be taken home; they are perfect when washed. Those with a hole through them are considered especially lucky, representing the third, clairvoyant eye and the evil eye that wards off harm. Shells can also be used. A couple dozen similar and different colored stones or shells will give a prediction. ¶ Place a candle on a table and randomly scatter the stones around the front and sides of the candle. Light the wick and switch off any lights. Close your eyes for a few moments to attune yourself to the deeper levels of your psyche. When you open your eyes, the color of the first stone you are drawn to reveals an answer. Afterward, squint and look at the rays of candlelight. A beam pointing at a stone also has a message for you. If you allow the candle to burn for an hour or two, close your eyes, open them, and squint again, and more predictions will shine through. ¶ If the predominant color of the stone is:

✸ RED ✸

A flame is burning brightly in a lover's heart. To discover who loves
you so passionately, dwell on the stone or light beam shining upon
the stone until the amorous person's name springs to mind.

✸ BROWN ✸

A slowly developing relationship, barely visible in winter,
will amaze you in spring. A special someone
will declare a love for you.

✸ YELLOW ✸

In the sunshine of the summer months, love will make you
laugh and smile. You will share sunny days with
someone who has a warm, caring heart.

✸ GREEN ✸

A love interest will quickly grow during
the spring and summer. Green, an emblem of nature, predicts
that you should wait as nature does, have faith,
and let nature unfailingly take its course and surprise you.

✸ BLUE ✸

Blue skies of happiness are forecast.
Lighter, brighter, sunnier days are beginning and
will continue to shine for you.

✸ VIOLET ✸

A hidden truth that you discover will shine
a light of happiness and relief when confirmed.

✸ BLACK ✸

Expect a sad love ending for someone,
but not necessarily you.

Candle flame divination

Light any colored candle and switch off the lights in the room. Sit with the candle, close your eyes to clear your mind, open them, and study the flame.

- *A rising flame signifies that you are the flame burning in another's heart.*
- *A long, narrow flame means the arrival of a new lover for you.*
- *A flame flickering from side to side predicts a long journey involving love.*
- *A particularly bright flame means love is about to brighten your life with a happy surprise.*
- *A luminous glow at the tip of the wick means someone is thinking lovingly about you.*
- *Sparks reveal that sparks will fly in or around a love match.*
- *A falling flame means someone who is emitting mixed signals is undecided.*
- *A sputtering flame signifies the course of true love will not run smoothly.*
- *A flame that dies before the candle has burned through means the enlightened end of a bond, but not necessarily your relationship with the love of your life. It brings to light another's deceit and warns of a shocking discovery. One you trust may accidentally reveal secrecy and deception, but you will forgive the indiscretion.*

Does he or she love me?

Concentrate on your question while staring at clouds. Tell the clouds to answer yes to your question by dispersing. If the clouds part within a few minutes, blue skies of happiness are yours. Your desired truly loves you. Clouds that eventually part reveal that a separation will result in a union. Clouds that refuse to part show that temporary obstacles cloud the path of true love.

Twelve-candle circle

On a fine day or evening, take twelve candles out- doors with a group of friends. On concrete or other flat ground, disperse the candles evenly to form a circle about nine feet by twelve feet in diameter. Name any of the twelve candles to represent any potential lovers you or your friends desire. ¶ Light the twelve candles, then jump over each in a clockwise direc-tion. If a candle that represents a lover is extin-guished, it is a sign that the magical spark of love will not occur or that love light will fade and burn out. But a candle that stays lit is a sign of a happy love affair for you with that person. Relight any extin-guished candles so the next person can take a turn at jumping. ¶ Twelve candles set in a circle can also determine what love hopes and wishes lie in store during the next twelve months. Each candle represents a month of the year. ¶ Light the twelve candles, beginning with January and ending with December. Jump over them in a clockwise motion. The happiest months for you will be those revealed by candles that remain lit. The same twelve candles can be used to determine in which months you will marry. ¶ Seven of the twelve candles placed in a circle can prophesy on what day of the week you will meet or hear from your lover. The candles must be jumped over in a clockwise direction. Candles that remain lit are the brightest days for love. ¶ For "Seven Days of the Week Divination," you can use colored candles that represent each day of the week. These are:

          SUNDAY: *Orange*
          MONDAY: *White*
          TUESDAY: *Red*
          WEDNESDAY: *Yellow*
          THURSDAY: *Purple*
          FRIDAY: *Blue*
          SATURDAY: *Green*

Sow several seeds in a pot of soil to represent anticipated events.

Place the pot on a windowsill so that each seed obtains the same amount of sunshine. Water the seeds equally. The first seedling

Gambling with dice

Tumbling the die gives a random answer. One die has six possible answers that should reinforce your own judgment.

✺ ONE ✺

Stay as you are. Being prepared to go it alone will ultimately bring an addition to your benefit.

✺ TWO ✺

You are destined to meet someone special.

✺ THREE ✺

Either you or your lover thinks that you are each other's "one and only."

[49]

✺ FOUR ✺

Your own doubts are stronger than your lover's words and promised actions. You will make the right decision.

✺ FIVE ✺

If there are three people involved in a situation, trust yourself to walk away and wait. If love is true, your lover will join you; if not, you have a clear path ahead.

✺ SIX ✺

You will win your relationship wish.

to appear reveals which event will occur first. The last seedling to show represents which adventure will develop last.

He loves me,
He loves me not

Cut two one-inch squares from a piece of white paper. Color one square on the back and front with a black pen. Drop the white and the black square from a table. The one you love loves you too if the white square lands first. The answer is negative if the black square lands first.

Will we date?

Crack a walnut into two unbroken halves, and remove the nut. A walnut is a sign of fertility. To see whether or not the one you love will return or ask you out, secure a birthday candle in each walnut shell with melted candle wax. Float the shells in a fair sized bowl of water and light both candles, one to represent you and the other to symbolize your lover. If the shells float toward each other, you will date. If the shells drift apart, the one you love lacks interest. You can also use multiple walnut shells and candles if you are interested in more than one person. Shells that drift toward the shell representing you reveal who will approach you for a date. The candle that burns the longest represents the one whose love is strongest.

Hearing doves coo means your lover is talking about you

To be Kissed

Bring a rose petal along when you meet your love. When he or she is drinking from a cup or glass, notice where his or her lips touch the rim. Press a rose petal against the rim to imprint the invisible magnetism created by the lips of the one you love. Place the petal inside a new, white envelope and sleep with it under your pillow.

Will I hear from the one I love?

Place a wide-rimmed bowl on a table. Fill the bowl almost to the brim with water. Light a white candle beside the bowl. Ask your question and drop a pebble into the water. Count the ripples the pebble makes. An odd number of ripples answers yes. An even number of ripples answers no. ¶ If the answer is yes, you can then determine how many days or weeks it will take for your desired to contact you by asking: "Will it be in one day?" The answer is yes if the number of ripples is odd and no if even. If the answer is no, you can ask about time, or any other question, by the same method.

and wants to invite you to his or her home.

To get an errant lover
to return

Using a pin, inscribe your lover's name on a candle.
The candle should be of any color that your lover
predominantly wore at your last meeting. Inscribe
your name on a candle that is your favorite color.
Light both candles and sit with them while they
burn. ¶ In blue ink on white paper, write your
sweetheart's name, surrounded by a square. As the
candles melt, pour wax from both onto the letters,
saying: *"[Name of person]'s love for me is sealed."* When the
name is covered in wax and the wax is dry, place the
piece of paper in a new envelope to keep. Your lover
will return, unless the wax cracks.

To go out together

Collect rose petals after the dew has disappeared on
a warm day. Place all but one of the rose petals on
white paper to dry the moisture. The petals will need
turning to dry completely. On the remaining rose
petal, prick your name above your sweetheart's name
with a pin. ¶ Pour the other petals into a handkerchief and sprinkle them with powdered orrisroot,
mixing and crumbling the two together until you
have a fine powder. Put the still-whole petal bearing
your names on top of the mixture. Scoop the ingredients into a ball shape and tie a red ribbon around
them. Sleep with the spell pouch under your pillow
and you will not be alone for much longer.

Love written in the sands of time

Geomancy—"geo" derived from the Greek meaning *Earth* and "mancy," or *fortune-telling*—can answer romantic dilemmas. Pour sand an inch deep and leveled flat on a tea tray. A dinner plate placed on a tablecloth or newspaper will work too. Using just your fingertips, hold a pencil over the sand. Close your eyes while you or someone else counts to twenty-one, and allow your hand to be guided to draw shapes in the sand. Let the pencil feel as if it is guiding your hand.

[53]

- ᠙ LINES: *Short and separate lines reveal a lack of communication that will pass after a period of waiting. Short, deep lines foretell an unexpected visitor's arrival. Long, deep lines forecast a long journey involving a love affair far from home or traveling far together. Jagged lines depict many ups and downs before the course of true love runs smoothly.*
- ᠙ LETTERS: *Seeing letters predicts these answers: D: Definitely, M: Maybe, N: No, P: Perhaps, Y: Yes.*
- ᠙ A LARGE CROSS: *A happy love affair is predicted. The deeper the cross, the truer and more visible are a lover's sentiments for you.*
- ᠙ SMALL CIRCLE: *You will be introduced and welcomed into your lover's family circle. A friendship or engagement ring may follow.*

⁊ **LARGE CIRCLE:** *Your circle of friends and acquaintances is growing. You will visit unknown locations that continue to expand your social life.*

⁊ **TRIANGLE:** *Love is looking up if the triangle is facing upward. Pointing downward predicts that delays, separation, and difficulties will hamper a meeting of two hearts.*

⁊ **SQUARE:** *Happy surprises and gifts will exceed your expectations in another's home.*

⁊ **HEART:** *A happy, enduring love affair is forecast.*

⁊ **BIRDS:** *You will soon receive news or an invitation.*

⁊ **MOUNTAIN:** *Pleasure is about to result from passing an exam or rising above a difficult time.*

[54]

⁊ **SEA:** *You will soon travel or receive news from overseas, from afar, or from the coast. A seaside trip is forecast.*

⁊ **SWORD:** *You are in someone's heart. Passion will appear.*

⁊ **A FLOWER:** *A gift of appreciation will be given to you.*

Sneezing on a Saturday foretells an unexpected visit or news from your lover on Sunday.

magical
times

Certain dates and times of year are especially potent for love. Aligning yourself to such persuasive opportunities can make getting what you want simple. Spring, Midsummer Night, Halloween, Christmas, New Year's Eve, and new and full moons are all especially persuasive times for passion.

Your magical abracadabra hour

Since we are a part of nature, our personal strength waxes and wanes similarly to the moon phases and the growth and decline of the fruits of the earth. There is one morning and one evening hour of every day when your unique power is at its height. It is your personal magical hour. To discover your spellbinding hour, add up the month, date, and year of your birth.

DATE OF BIRTH: September 17, 1982
MONTH: September is the ninth month 9
DATE: 17, 1 + 7 = 8 8
YEAR: 1982, 1 + 9 + 8 + 2 = 20, 2 + 0 = 2 2
9 + 8 + 2 = 19, 1 + 9 = 10 10

Ten o'clock in the morning and ten o'clock in the evening are both personal potent hours for weaving magic and winning success in your everyday dealings. If you know your lover's date of birth, you can very easily link into your beloved's psyche by casting your love spell at his or her magical hour, derived by the same formula.

Moon love

Each new moon is a magical time for spell casting to attract love. A new-moon spell should be cast when the new moon can be seen as a growing crescent in the sky. It should not be cast in the dark of the moon, three days before it is visible in the sky. A wanion is a spell cast at the waning of the moon to remove negativity. The ebb and flow of the moon is the ebb and flow of the tide. The moon rules receptivity by reflecting light from the sun. The full moon is an unsettled time when changes take place. Arrangements go awry and oppositions occur because human life seems to feel the conflicting forces taking place between the sun and the moon. On the night of a full moon, the moon's magnetism with the earth pulls the sea upward in a peak toward the moon, a tidal wave is created, and the tide of the sea turns.

Lunar lime bath

Lime, sacred to the love planet, can attract love. Begin your spell on the morning after a new moon. For the next twenty-eight days, sprinkle five drops of lime oil or pure lime juice into your bath or shower water. To attract someone you see daily, rub an additional five drops of lime oil into a piece of paper bearing that person's name. Carry the piece of paper with you during the day.

Drawing down the moon

"Drawing down the moon" is seeing a reflection of the moon in any form of water (a pond, a puddle, the sea) or a mirror. You can use a bowl of water or a hand mirror to draw down the moon and cast moon magic. On the night of a full moon, cut a circle from a piece of clean, white paper to represent the full moon. In ink, write the name of your lover backwards on the moon shape and place it in front of a mirror. Write your own name backward on the reverse side. The one you love will love you in return.

Moonlight magic

In front of a mirror or on top of a flat mirror, light a silver or white candle to represent the moon. Cut a crescent-moon shape out of a leaf. Place it flat in front of the candle, with the points facing left. Write your name on one side of the moon-shaped leaf and your lover's name on the reverse. If your spell can be cast where moonlight catches the mirror, you have drawn down the moon to win the heart of the one you love. Turn the leaf over to reflect your name, and your lover's heart will be turned to you. ¶ Sleep with the leaf under your pillow until the next full moon, then tear it into tiny pieces. Scatter them into a shower of rain or toss them into a stream, a river, the sea, or other flowing water.

A moon-cycle
meeting

To bring a reunion within the following twenty-eight days, cut a pear in half. Place the two halves together and bind them as one with twine. Light a pink candle and say: *"We are one."* Bake the pear and eat it while thinking of the two of you together.

Moon roses
for constant love

When the moon is full, place two roses in a vase, one to represent you and the other to symbolize the one you love. Place the roses in front of your dressing-table mirror and light a candle so that the roses and flame reflect in the mirror. Your spell will be most potent if the mirror reflects the moon. Think of you and your lover together, happy in love. Snuff out the candle and love will bloom. ¶ The candle can be relit beside the roses when you wish to send a strong love thought to the one you love. When the roses fade, keep the petals in an envelope that he or she has sent to you. Or use a new envelope to keep under your pillow or in a bedside drawer.

While your lover is sleeping, use a hand mirror to reflect moonlight onto your sweetheart's face. Close your eyes,

Moon roses
love

A few days before or on the night of a full moon, take a hand mirror, two roses, and a red or pink ribbon outside. Hold the mirror up to catch the moon's reflection and place the roses on top of the moon's image. Bind the roses to the mirror with the ribbon. Place the mirror and roses at your bedside. When the roses fade, scatter the petals in your bathwater to absorb love.

New moon
love attraction

On a Friday night when the moon is new, light a red candle. Write the name of the one you desire on a small piece of red paper. Rub rose oil into the paper. Burn the paper in the flame while saying: *"It is not this name I wish to burn, but [name of person]'s heart I wish to turn. May [name of person] neither sleep nor rest find, until [name of person] comes to me and speaks his/her mind."* Leave the paper to extinguish to ash in a saucer. Snuff out the candle and go to bed without uttering a word.

wish your wish, and the one you love will be spellbound by the charm.

A full-moon wish

Preferably outdoors, hold a glass of water up to the moon so that it reflects into the water. Close your eyes, make your wish, and drink all the water while wishing all the bad things in your relationship to pass away with the flow of the moon. The waning moon will carry all negative emotions away.

Mirror magic wishes

A hand mirror is an emblem of truth. All mirrors symbolize imagination and are believed to contain and absorb images. Just as your soul is said to be projected in a mirror image, so too is the essence of the stars. ¶ On a starry night, stand outdoors or indoors by a window with a hand mirror held to reflect the sky. Reflect seven stars in the mirror on seven consecutive nights, and make your wish on each of the seven stars.

To attract a summer of love, as well as the sunshine of love, grow St. John's Wort close to your front door. It is a common herb with yellow flowers that bloom on the longest day of the year, June 21.

Dream mirror magic

To dream of your next partner, take a bath, then light a candle. Look into the flame before getting into bed and hold a hand mirror to reflect the flame. Snuff out the candle. Sleep with the mirror under your pillow and you will dream of the one who will ignite the flames of passion in your heart.

Sunshine
for a special day

To represent the sun, wind a red ribbon around a pebble until the pebble is completely concealed. Bind the ribbon with a knot. By touching the pebble, you establish a psychic link with the tiny electrons whizzing inside it. This extension of your mind will bring wish fulfillment. ¶ On a yellow piece of paper, write the date on which you wish the sun to shine. Place the pebble on top of the paper on a windowsill and leave it there. After the date, burn or bury the paper and keep the pebble for future sunny days.

To summon
the winds of change

To invoke a breeze, pour water from a height so that it splashes on a stone. Speak or think your wish as the water falls in showers.

Hot summer days will bring a surprise of summer love.

To cloud the sunset

Pick up a handful of sand, earth, or dandelion down. Scatter it into the air and blow it toward the sun while wishing for the evening to close.

Valentine's Day divination

Valentine's Day is dedicated to lovers because birds begin to pair on that special date. To predict what your next partner will be like, ask a little bird to tell you. The first bird you see on Valentine's Day is symbolic of your current or next love.

- **ROBIN**: *Your future partner is a proud home-bird.*
- **GOLDEN COLORED BIRD**: *He/she is rich.*
- **STARLING**: *He/she is greedy.*
- **SPARROW**: *He/she is trusting.*
- **BLACKBIRD**: *He/she adores music.*
- **CROW OR RAVEN**: *He/she is jealous.*
- **SEAGULL**: *He/she lives on the coast.*
- **BRIGHTLY COLORED BIRD**: *He/she is a larger-than-life character.*
- **THRUSH**: *He/she has true feelings for you.*
- **DOVE OR ANY WHITE BIRD**: *A marriage proposal is represented and you will soon marry.*
- **DUCK**: *Any bird with webbed feet reveals he/she will be difficult to hang on to.*

If the Valentine's Day bird flies to the right, your relationship will soar to happy heights; to the left signifies that the course of true love may not run smoothly and may take some time to get off the ground. Birds flying toward the east are a good omen for new love because the sun rises in the east. Birds flying toward the west and the sunset represent heartache. Birds flying hither and thither represent agitations and uncertainty in love. A steady, horizontal flight designates strong, purposeful love.

Valentine's day divination with friends

[65]

With a group of friends, write the names of each potential suitor on small pieces of paper. Drop the male and female names into separate paper bags. Everyone present should draw three names from the bag in which they have placed their pieces of paper. Each time, the piece of paper chosen should then be returned to the bag. If a person draws the same name three times, it is a sure sign of a future relationship with the named person.

Toss feathers in the air or sprinkle tiny pieces of white paper from a window to send your heartfelt wishes and settle differences in your favor.

Springtime
magic

Easter is the first Sunday after the first full moon, which rises after March 21, the spring equinox. Spring love spells are especially potent, as they are harmonious and in sympathy with nature. Therefore, spring will have the same effect on the one you love as it has on nature. Impatience for a spell to materialize does not mean the spell is not working. Like spring, love may be hidden in the darkness of the cold soil before it bursts open. Lack of faith and interference can unbalance delicate, subtler forces that, like nature, are working invisibly.

Halloween
dream divination

Chop one walnut, one hazelnut, one almond, and one brazil nut. Add seven pinches of ground nutmeg. Break a slice of bread into seven small pieces. Dab each piece into the mixture and form each into a little ball. Eat the bread upon going to bed. You will dream of your lover or lover to be.

To see an apparition of your future partner, slice an apple into nine segments. Put the segments on a skewer. Hold the skewer over your left shoulder while looking

To make three wishes
come true

On Halloween, bury three hyacinth bulbs in an indoor pot. Each bulb represents a wish that you would like to see fulfilled. Make your wishes as you plant each bulb. Place three very small stones above each bulb to distinguish each wish. Place the pot in a permanent position in your bedroom. ¶ As the bulbs grow, your wishes will take root. As the leaves sprout, your wishes will begin to grow. When the hyacinths bloom, your wishes will come true according to the order of which grows first, second, or third. The scent and appearance of each bloom will reveal how sweetly your wish will be fulfilled. When the flowers fade, replant the bulbs outdoors.

[67]

Halloween
marriage divination
with friends

Those who wish to know who will marry first should each thread an apple on a string through the core. The string should be knotted at the base of the core. The suspended apples should then be spun in a circular movement. The person whose apple drops first will be the first to marry.

into a candlelit mirror on the stroke of midnight. A ghostly vision will appear in the mirror.

Yule divination

On Christmas Eve, walk backward to an apple tree, then walk forward around the tree nine times. Close your eyes for a few moments, then open them to see a misty vision of your future partner.

A Christmas candle wish

On Christmas Eve, inscribe a candle with your wish or wishes. Light the candle on each of the twelve days of Christmas, and on each day, snuff the candle out. On the last night, January 6, bury the candle after snuffing it out.

[68]

A New Year's Eve wish

Make sure your back door is open just before midnight. Place several coins on a windowsill and bind together one holly sprig, one mistletoe sprig, and one ivy stem with red ribbon. Wish your wish while opening your front door at the witching hour of midnight. Old loves will be gone and a new and long-lasting love will be welcomed in. Close the doors if you wish to keep love in.

A New Year's Day
wish

On the first day of the new year, spread a large sheet of newspaper over a table and cover yourself with an apron or smock. Drop blue, green, red, or black ink or food coloring into a large glass bowl. Take a sprig of holly berries and carefully stir the ink in the bowl while wishing your special New Year's Day wish. Any ink that splashes on the newspaper or your hand is significant. The words, sentences, or paragraphs following the ink splashes are a forecast for the new year. Ink splashed on your skin may form an alphabetical shape representing a lover's initials or a place connected to him or her. Once you have seen these signs, carefully pour the ink away.

[69]

It is considered lucky to marry when it is snowing, because the wedding is truly a white wedding. Snowflakes are an omen of babies soon to be conceived.

love magic
for life

When two people have fallen in love, neither person wants to live his or her life without the other. Both want to share their lives, so marriage is a natural progression. Since the love link is already strong, spells for marriage work easily. Outside influences inevitably affect a relationship, but inner powers such as love, understanding, and sympathy strengthen a love bond, creating an energy field that repels harm.

To find a husband

If you are looking for a husband, call on St. Catherine, the patron saint of spinsters: *"I need a husband, St. Catherine; a handsome one, St. Catherine; a rich one, St. Catherine; and soon, St. Catherine."*

To receive a marriage proposal

On the night of a full moon or a few days before, use a pin to inscribe a small gold candle with the name of the one you wish to marry, followed by *"will propose to [your name]."* Place it in front of your bedroom mirror and light the wick so that the mirror reflects both the candle and its flame. Sit with the candle while it expires and extinguishes of its own accord. Any candle remnants should be buried in salt.

To get him
to propose

Using a pin, write your beloved's name on a red candle. Inscribe your name on another red candle. In an old saucepan, heat the candles to liquid wax. When the wax has cooled and is beginning to solidify, remove the two wicks. Scoop about half the wax out of the pan to mold a figure that represents the one you love with the arms outstretched. Use the remainder of the wax to make a figure that represents you. Place the figures face-to-face in an embracing position and tie them in place with a red ribbon. Light a red candle and write the following on a bay leaf, using a pin or pen: "[name of person] will propose to me." Place the bay leaf and figures in a new white envelope and seal the envelope. Snuff out the candle and keep the envelope close to you.

[74]

To get him
to propose

Midsummer Night's Eve (June 20) is magical because it is the eve of the longest day of the year—the summer solstice. On Midsummer Night's Eve, light a gold candle, take a new piece of pink paper, and in gold ink write your first name in cursive writing connected to your lover's first and last name, forming a circle like a gold wedding ring. Sprinkle rose oil onto the names, then smudge them together until they merge. Hold the piece of paper in your left hand, between your wedding-ring finger and little finger, and move the piece of paper forward, backward, and forward above the flame so that the fire heats the rose oil and sends a rose aroma into the atmosphere. Place the piece of paper under your pillow and snuff out the candle. A Midsummer Night's Eve dream will pervade your sleep. Keep the envelope under your pillow and your intended will always be attracted to appear in your dreams.

Cloud counting

When the moon is full, stand outdoors with a hand mirror to reflect the moon. Once it is captured, begin counting the seconds until a cloud appears across the moon in the mirror. Each second counted represents a month or a year. The second when a cloud touches the moon represents how many months or years will pass before marriage.

To marry

Alone or with the one you wish to marry, close your eyes and imagine the marriage ceremony and exchanging vows. Picture your wedding details as clearly as possible.

It is believed to be unlucky to marry on your birthday.

To keep a couple happy

On the night of a new moon, place straw in water to soak and soften for a few days. When the straw is pliable, tie and knot strands of it together until it is long enough to tie around two trees. ¶ When the straw begins to disintegrate, bury it between the trees. The health of your marriage will be dictated by the health of the trees.

[76]

"Tie the knot" on your wedding day by tying a strand of the groom's clothes to a thread of the bride's clothing. The threads kept as a love amulet are said to be an eternal marriage bond.

Keeping
LOVE
alive

Keeping love alive means continually being aware of your lover's needs by trying to please and adapt to circumstances to suit both partners. Although two people will always have different views and will never agree all the time, they can merge and blend into one relationship by striving together to meet their own idea of happiness.

To make love grow

To keep a new love thriving, sprinkle a handful of rice, a handful of parsley seeds, and a handful of sesame seeds into a bowl. Using your fingers, stir them seven times in a clockwise direction, then scatter them on the ground early in the morning. ¶ Another method is to use a pomegranate, a symbol long associated with fertility because it is full of red seeds. Pierce a red candle with a pin so that the pin tip emerges on the opposite side of the candle. Light the candle. Take a pomegranate and stick pins into it in the shape of letters that spell your lover's name. Snuff out the candle and bury the pomegranate.

To bring the flame
of your life safely home,
    keep a lighted candle on
a windowsill while your loved
one journeys to your door.

To preserve love

Ginger is a preservative. To preserve a suitor's passion for you, place his or her photograph facing a mirror with a ginger root beside it and light a red candle. Your lover's passion for you will double while the spell ingredients are reflected in the mirror. Think hard and reflect your thoughts through the flame and photograph and into the mirror image.

Flower vitality

Pick flowers at midnight on a full moon and lay them side by side, touching each other, in front of your dressing-table mirror or at your bedside. If the flowers have faded by morning, love is fading too. Place the flowers in a vase of water. The flame of love can be and will be rekindled if the flowers regain their vitality.

To bewitch with a kiss

When you are being kissed, imagine the two of you encircled by silver light. Visualize the circle growing brighter, wider, and stronger with the sweet kiss. When you part company, visualize the circle around your lover alone. In your absence, others who find him or her attractive will only get as far as flirting because you have cast your protective spell.

[80]

To drive your lover
wild with passion

On a Friday night at five to twelve, light a red candle. Heat an old knife with a wooden handle over the flame. Use neither a good knife, because it may incur a mark, nor a metal-handled knife, because it will burn your hand and anything else you may drop the knife on to. At the stroke of midnight and when the blade is red hot, say: *"[name of person]'s passion is red hot. To me he/she turns when love burns."* Plunge the blade into a deep metal bowl of cold water and snuff out the candle.

To hold on to love

When the moon is waxing, plant two miniature roses in one pot large enough for two plants to grow. Tie and knot a pink ribbon around the two rose plants. You may need to loosen the ribbon so that the plants always look comfortably bound. ¶ As the roses grow, their roots will entwine, binding you and your lover. When the leaves grow, love will grow. When the petals open, love will beckon, and when the roses bloom, so too will you and your love. When the roses fade, remove the ribbon and keep the plants alive.

To see a robin or rainbow on your birthday or wedding day is a lucky love sign.

To keep love true

Anoint a blue candle with clove oil by sprinkling a few drops from the candle tip, which symbolizes the North Pole, to the candle's center. Sprinkle a few more drops of clove oil from the candle base's South Pole toward the center. Cloves, a natural preservative, can enhance, defend, and conserve when called upon. ¶ Take a bay leaf—ruled by the sun—and, using a pen, inscribe your lover's name upon it. Sprinkle and rub a few drops of clove oil over the name to preserve his or her love for you. ¶ When the candle wax has melted, pour the liquid over the name written on the bay leaf. Your lover's heart will soften for you and become strong again as the wax solidifies. While pouring the wax over the name, say: *"Your love for me is sealed."* ¶ Place the bay leaf in your bedroom, either on the windowsill, where the sun shines to represent daylight and love light, or in a bedroom drawer, symbolizing nights together. Move the bay leaf to different locations as needed to strengthen your day or evening needs.

[82]

Ivy clings to what it grows on, so it symbolizes your lover, encouraging him or her to hang on to you and your love. Wind ivy around honeysuckle and bind it in place with red ribbon or cord.

To bind love
with honeysuckle

Honeysuckle, known as the "witch's ladder," is renowned for helping love to climb onward and upward to heavenly heights. Cut seven stems of honeysuckle with or without flowers. Using a pin, inscribe a red candle with your lover's name, writing from the candle base up toward the wick. Be sure to leave space at the base for a holder. Take a red ribbon or cord about thirteen inches long. Place each of the seven stems flat on the table in front of the candle, as if they were rungs on a ladder. Tie the bottom stem to the second, securing them together with a double knot. Continue to bind all seven stems, each with a double knot, while saying (according to the appropriate knot): *"My spell is begun by knot one. It is coming true, tied by knot two. Knot number three binds [name of person] to me. Knot four opens love's door. Knot five proves love thrives. Knot six, this spell will fix. By knot seven, this spell is blessed by heaven."* ¶ Snuff out the candle. Keep your witch's ladder close to you to ensure your lover's affections stay attached to you. As time goes by, tighten the knots and straighten the rungs to keep him or her in line with your rising aspirations and coupling expectations.

[83]

Place them together in a vase.
When the honeysuckle fades, bury it
together with the ivy.

To share
the same dream

Decide with your absent lover to dream of a future special occasion the two of you will attend. Synchronize your bedtimes for the same hour on the same day of the week. Both of you should light a purple candle for half an hour before going to bed. ¶ One person may dream the premonition before the other, but by repeating the formula, both of you will dream, perhaps on the same night. Tell each other your dreams and watch as the events seen in the dream transpire.

[84]

To bewitch a lover

By candlelight, place into a dish about half an ounce each of orrisroot, sandalwood, and talcum powder. Blend the three together with your fingertips. Funnel the blend into a vial or white envelope and snuff the candle out. A pinch of this powder placed in your lover's pocket will keep your desired true to you.

Seeing a pair of doves is
a romantic omen that love is in
the air and a cozy love nest
will be yours.

A recipe
for happy love

Pick, cut, and boil two apples together with your lover, using the same spoon to stir and mingle your wishes. Put the mixing spoon aside and share a silver-colored spoon to eat the apples together. Apples are ruled by the love planet, Venus; silver and emotions are ruled by the moon.

To prevent
forgetfulness

Place a large bunch of forget-me-nots in a glass vase on top of a piece of paper bearing the name of the one you love. If you have your lover's signature, use it. Light a pink candle beside the vase and will him or her toward you as you look into the flame.

To never say
good-bye

On a small piece of paper, write the last words he or she spoke to you when you last parted. Place that piece of paper in a clean, white envelope, along with a few fresh sage leaves or a sprinkling of dried sage. Sage, ruled by Venus, will secure your new lover's spoken words and keep them true while you possess the magical ingredients. To reverse the spell, burn the envelope and its contents and bury the ash, or cast it outside to the winds of change.

To be part of
your lover

Pick a rose petal and prick your lover's name in the petal with a pin. Roll the petal inside a heart-shaped piece of rice paper and give it to your lover to eat.

To keep two hearts
as one

To prevent the heartstrings of two hearts that beat as one from being severed, twine rosemary around closed scissors. Rosemary, ruled by the sun, represents happy memories. Bury the scissors with the cutting point directed away from your home, but not in the direction of your lover's home (if you live separately). ¶ Should you wish to end this relationship in the future, dig up the scissors, untwine the rosemary, open the scissors, and bury them in the compass direction facing your lover's home while saying: "*[Name of person], go your way, free from my spell.*"

To form a lovers' pact, tear two washed rose petals and place them in two champagne glasses. Fill both glasses to the rim with sparkling springwater. Link left arms,

To be part of
the one you love

Inscribe your name with a pin on a fresh or dried bay leaf. Cook the bay leaf in a recipe that your lover will eat. Alternatively, inscribe a strawberry with your name. Place the strawberry in a fruit salad, making sure that he or she is the one who eats the strawberry.

To melt a partner's
heart with love

Take a pink candle, and with a pin, inscribe these words: *"[Name of person]'s heart will melt with love for me."* Place the candle on top of a flat mirror that is positioned to cast the moon's reflection. ¶ Place an ice cube in a small saucer beside the candle on the mirror. Sit with the candle and watch the ice melt to water. As the candle and ice melt together, your beloved's heart will melt for you. When the candle has burned through the inscription, flick a few drops of ice water onto the flame with your fingertips to snuff it out. Pour the remaining water onto a plant.

with the glasses held in the left hands
Both must drink the petals
and water while wishing.

To kindle the flames
of passion

Friday is the day of the week ruled by Venus, the planet of love, so cast this spell on a Friday night. Light a red candle beside a photograph of the one you love. If you do not have a photograph, strongly visualize the one you adore. Release three droplets of rose oil onto the flame and pierce the candle an inch from the top with a pin, going all the way through the wick while saying: *"The flame of passion I ignite, in [name of person]'s heart by candlelight. As I pierce the candle wick, his/her love for me I fix."* Once the candle has burned down past the pin, snuff it out.

To seal two lovers
as one

Light a red candle to represent the one you love and a yellow candle to symbolize yourself. Cut out two paper heart shapes or use confetti hearts. Write your lover's name on one heart and your name on the other. Position the hearts so that the two names face each other. Pour melted wax over the hearts to seal the two as one. Your lover's heart will be bonded to you in love and your heart will be united to your partner's. Place the hearts in a new envelope and store in a bedroom drawer for safekeeping. Snuff out the candle.

To spice up your love life

Light a white candle. Wash your hands thoroughly. Place seven pinches of nutmeg and seven pinches of cloves into your cupped left hand and sprinkle in some salt until your palm is full. Cup your right hand over your left and sit, holding the concoction for a few minutes. Pour the mixture into a piece of clean, white paper and fold the edges to seal the contents. Hold the sachet to your heart, then place it under your pillow. Snuff out the candle. ¶ When meeting the one you love, carry the sachet close to your heart. At the moment when you want to add a little magic, open the packet and sprinkle a few pinches where your lover will sit or walk. Close the sachet and keep it undetected. On returning home, sleep with the packet under your pillow to use again, until the contents of the sachet are exhausted. When the packet is empty, burn it in the flame of a white candle and drop the burning paper into a dish to extinguish.

To ward off the flirting green eyes of jealousy, cross your fingers when someone takes a fancy to your lover.

To keep love sweet

Write the name of the one you love in red ink on a tiny piece of pink paper. Take a small jar of honey, and using a spoon, immerse the piece of paper in the honey. Replace the lid. Put the honey pot beside a pink candle and light the candle. As the flame burns, say: *"Honey is sweet and so is he/she, [name of person's] love will stick to me."* Snuff out the candle and keep the honey jar.

A lovers' knot

[90]

To bind two lovers' hearts, twist and knot together one length of purple cord and one length of yellow cord. Place the love amulet on your partner's wrist and knot the two loose ends to form a bracelet. Weave the same colored cords to make a bracelet for yourself, or ask your lover to do so. Either way the one you love must tie the knot on your left wrist, because that wrist is closest to your heart.

To stumble on a staircase you are ascending is a sign that marriage is much closer than you think.

To keep your lover
true to you

Take a pair of your lover's pants. Place a pair of your own pants on top, and wrap the two pairs up to make a parcel that is as small as possible. ¶ Take a length of red ribbon to represent him or her and a similar length of yellow ribbon to represent you. Tie the red ribbon lengthwise and the yellow ribbon widthwise to represent your power over the person. Tie both ribbons together in a lovers' knot—a knot that has two loops, one red, one yellow. Form a figure eight, a symbol representing every ending being followed by a new beginning. Also tie the loose ends, going from yellow to red and red to yellow, in that order. The three knots together represent both the male and the female. Keep the charm under your pillow or in one of your bedroom drawers. ¶ If you are unable to procure a pair of pants, use a pair of socks, or one sock, a T-shirt, gloves, or even a handkerchief. As long as your spell uses an item belonging to the one you desire, that ingredient will help grant your wish.

Another marriage sign is
unexpectedly finding a pin
in your clothes.

To make your lover
rampant with desire

Find a stone with a hole through it. Write your suitor's name in red ink on a small piece of red paper. Tie the piece of paper into a scroll shape with red thread, then insert the paper through the hole in the stone. Keep the "love stone" as a love amulet. To recharge its energy, place the charm beside a lit red candle or on a windowsill where moonlight will shine upon it. To reverse the spell, remove the scrolled paper and bury both the paper and the stone in separate places.

To keep your lover
honest

Take an empty, sterilized jar. Sprinkle in thirteen pins, fill the jar with boiling water, and leave it to cool. Secure the lid. Dig a hole seven inches deep and put the jar into the earth, with the glass end pointing in the compass direction of your lover's home. An indoor pot of earth will work just as well. ¶ Leave the jar alone until you want a stronger reaction. Then exhume the glass jar, shake it, and rebury it. By their natural magnetic alignment, the pins inside the jar will point you in the direction of your true destiny and carry you there.

To hold on to love

When sitting outside with your lover, pick up a stone and place the stone where the person's figure casts a shadow on the ground. Leave the stone in the shadow for as long as possible. Afterward keep the stone close to you. Having retained part of your lover's essential being, the stone will help you to capture his or her heart.

To keep love true

Place a few strands of your beloved's hair on a small piece of paper. Place a sprig of fresh rosemary and a sprig of fresh sage on top, or sprinkle the piece of paper with dried rosemary and sage. Roll the paper and contents into a scroll shape. Tie the scroll with green ribbon to represent fertility and keep it close to you. Renew the scroll and ingredients twelve months later to revitalize the charm.

To entice passion

For passion, inscribe the name of the one you desire in a circle around a red candle, using a pin. Light the candle. Pour a little coriander into your left hand, and with your right hand, throw a few pinches into the flame while the candle burns through the inscription.

To turn romantic
love into
red-hot passion

With a pin, inscribe your lover's name in cursive writing on a strawberry. Then inscribe your name as a continuation. ¶ In red ink on white paper, write your name in cursive writing, with his name continuing from yours in a circular shape. Rub the strawberry into the names written on the piece of paper. Being red, a strawberry represents passion, life, and blood. ¶ Leave the paper to dry, then burn it in a candle flame. Allow the paper to extinguish to ash in a dish. Snuff out the candle and bury it with the ash and strawberry remains.

To heal a lovers' tiff

Light a blue candle. Hold a small amount of salt in your left hand. Using your right hand, throw a few pinches of salt into the flame. As the flame burns blue, healing has begun.

In early spring, sow sweet-pea seeds in a pot. In July, when the sweet peas flower, twine pairs of tendrils together to bind him or her to you. Like lovers, sweet peas cling for support.

To bind two lovers

Take two potatoes that appear similar in shape to figures of people, one to represent you and the other to represent the one you love. Using a pin, inscribe a pink candle with your lover's name, followed by your own name. If married, write your maiden name. Place the spuds face-to-face, as if in an embracing position, and bind them together with red ribbon. ¶ Allow the candle to burn though the inscription before snuffing it out. Bury the potatoes under an apple tree or close to a rose bush, because apple and rose are sacred to the love planet, Venus.

To protect a loving relationship

Find a large, hollow oak tree that is alive and flourishing. Oak, a symbol of strength and ruled by Jupiter—a planet of optimism—is a powerful protector. Like all trees, oak symbolizes a world axis. ¶ Find two stones, one to represent you and the other to symbolize the one you love. Place the stones so they are touching, side by side, on the ground against the oak. Cover the stones with leaves. ¶ Your and your lover's fates are connected to the destiny of the tree. If the tree is healthy, your love life will flourish. Should the tree grow ill, so too will your special relationship unless the stones are removed. If you wish to distance yourself from your lover, take the stone away that represents you.

Magic reflected

You can enhance a beloved's feelings toward you. When you have found love and want to hold on to it, dab the four corners of your lover's bedroom or bathroom mirror with a little rose oil. When your intended looks into the mirror, the person will see him or herself in a loving light that reflects you and draws you into his or her life.

To keep a rival away

Take a white candle to represent you and a blue candle to symbolize your lover. Also take a short gray-, neutral-, or black-colored candle to represent your love rival. Using a pin, inscribe your name, followed by your lover's name, on the candle that represents you. Inscribe your lover's name, followed by your name, on the candle symbolic of your beloved. On the candle representing your rival, inscribe only your rival's name and insert a pin through it, close to the top of the candle. ¶ Place the candles representing you and your partner side by side. Distance the rival candle by placing it as far away on the table as you can or in another safe place in the room. Light the first two candles and allow them to burn brightly before lighting the rival candle. When lighting the rival candle, say: *"[Name of person] go away today, and stay away."* Sit with the candles that represent you and your lover and bask in the flames' light.

Allow no thought of your rival to disturb the love light. Snuff the rival candle out and let the remaining two burn, moving them closer together so they touch; then snuff them out. Wrap the rival candle in an old postdated newspaper to represent the past tense. Pin the newspaper to the candle and quickly bury the package away from your home and your lover's—the further away the better.

For everlasting love

A yew tree is capable of living for more than a thousand years and is therefore a symbol of everlasting life. Take two yew sprigs, one to represent you and one to represent your lover. Bind them together with a length of blue and a length of yellow ribbon or cord, secured with a double knot. Place them in a clean, white envelope to keep among your personal possessions.

[97]

To never let love go

When you want to hold on to the one you love, you must find a tree that you particularly like in your garden or the countryside. Place a stone—to represent love—in the crook of a tree branch. Leave the stone in the tree. Some believe a tree is a spirit while others think it is a home for a tree spirit.

To chain a heart
to yours

Thread a needle with two lengths of different colored thread, one to represent his astrological sign and the other to symbolize your birth sign. (Or use red for passion and pink for love, or black and white.) ¶ Without letting your lover know, embroider a heart on an item of his or her clothing in chain stitch. To make a chain stitch, loop a piece of thread around the point of the needle. Pass one thread color under the needle's point and let the other color lie on top. Pull both threads. Work the next loop with the other color under the needle's point. When you are finished with the heart, encircle it by embroidering his or her name to join your name, beginning where your name ends and ending where your name begins. ¶ When both names are stitched, keep the talisman with you. To invoke the one you love, place the talisman beside a lit candle and call him or her to you. The link of love can only be broken when you undo the stitching, or burn or bury the love charm.

To hold on to the love of your life, place two red roses in a small jam jar. Fill the jar with sunflower oil and seal it with its lid. Bury the jar with the glass end

To keep love

Crack a walnut in half and remove the nut. Ruled by the sun, a walnut influences light to spread in darkness. Write your name above your lover's name in black ink on a small piece of white paper. Put the piece of paper in the shell's cavity and join the two halves together as one nutshell. Bind the package in place with a red ribbon or cord to represent life. Keep it as an amulet.

Love letters

Handwritten love letters carry the essence of the writer who has penned the words and touched the paper and envelope. Love letters should never be burned or thrown away unless you wish the love affair to end. To lose a love letter is a sign that you may lose the heart of the one you love. ¶ To receive two love letters from the same person in one day is a sign that you will receive good news before the day is over. If your handwriting is shaky when penning a love letter, it is a sign that you are loved. Blotted ink reveals that your lover thinks of you constantly and that you have blotted out his or her finer sensibilities. A love letter written in red ink is an omen of a quarrel. If you meet the postman when sending a love letter, it means that you are about to hear surprisingly good news. It is a sign that your and your

pointing in the compass
direction of his or her home.

lover's paths will soon cross if your love letters cross in the mail. ¶ To send or receive a love letter with a stamp that is not canceled means everlasting love. A deficiently stamped letter reveals a lack of commitment. A stamp stuck upside down is a sign that a relationship will turn your world upside down.

For everlasting love

In spring, when apple blossoms are in bloom, pick a few sprigs with a lover or friend. Using pink thread or ribbon, tie the blossom into two little bunches while saying: *"Winding and weaving, never deceiving, entwined together, our friendship lasts forever."* Place both apple-blossom bouquets in heart-shaped cookie cutters on a nonstick pan. ¶ Sit together and light as many candles as you can imagine years you will spend together. Pour hot liquid wax from two of the candles onto both bouquets while saying: *"Our two hearts are sealed as one. Love begun will never be undone."* ¶ When the two apple-blossom bouquets are completely covered with wax, add a few final drops while linking little fingers. When the wax hearts have cooled, snuff all the candles out and take one apple-blossom wax heart each to keep your two hearts as one forever. No matter what may happen in life, both of you will always be there for each other. The bond of love will exist in life and death and in the world beyond.

[100]

LOVE's
ups and downs

Familiarity with a person in a wrong relation-ship can make you wonder how you ever loved that person at all. When two people become close in mind or make love physically, their auras blend, engage, and enmesh. After you have made love, your partner's energy will stay with you for a while afterward and your energy will stay with your partner. When two auras part for everyday work or separate forever, an electrical radiance emanates from your inner self and your lover's inner self, extending beyond the physical and manifesting itself as an emotional, agonizing lovesickness. That is partly why making love with only the right person is so important. Two hearts and two bodies must be sincere to those they love. In both circumstances, parting will return you to your own aura but not to the original subtle emanation you had before your love affair. Because a relationship causes such an alteration, your or your lover's aura may take a while to recover and be whole again.

[103]

To discourage a love rival

Write the name of your rival in black ink on white paper. Place the paper underneath a heavy rock or stone to suppress the adversary's intentions to woo love away from you. The love you share with your desired will be free from jealousy or competition.

To put passion on ice

When the pace of love is too fast, too soon, you can cool your admirer's ardor with an ice cube. Write your lover's name on a small piece of paper. Place it face down in an ice-cube tray. Pour a little water and three drops of rose oil on top before freezing. ¶ When you are ready for passion, light a red candle inscribed with your lover's name. Place the ice cube in a dish in front of the candle and watch the flame melt the ice to water. Remove the piece of paper and let it dry to warm his heart to yours.

[104]

To say good-bye

After ending a love affair, write the name of your former sweetheart on a leaf or on a small piece of blue paper. To sever the past, walk backward to a river or the sea, with the leaf or piece of paper in your left hand. Toss the leaf or paper into the water over your left shoulder so that the named person flows out of your life. Avoid turning around or looking over your shoulder at any point, including when you walk away.

Light a candle and burn your
lover's signature in the flame.
A bright, narrow flame reveals that

To heal your
broken heart

Sprinkle three drops of chamomile oil into running bathwater. After bathing and dressing for bed, light a blue candle in front of a mirror and turn off any lights. Sit down and gaze into the mirror until you see your aura. It is a golden, silver, or white light about an inch above your head and shoulders, following the same contours. The light may be a foot or more wide. Imagine the golden, silver, or white light of your aura running like electricity in a clockwise circle around your body. ¶ Look into the flame's glow and notice which color you see first. That initial color is the healing color you personally need. Imagine it circulating like an electrical current about an inch around the outer contours of the golden, silver, or white light. ¶ After concentrating for a few moments on that circulating color, you will find that your aura is healed, but the fragility of all auras means the spell will need to be cast every night or regularly until you feel your heart is mended. You will notice that as you recover, your healing color will change. On each occasion end your spell by snuffing the candle out and getting straight into bed, where you will sleep peacefully and surprisingly well.

the person is in love with you.
a small, weak flame symbolizes weak affections.

To deter a love rival

Write the name of your rival in chalk on a small piece of black paper. Insert the piece of paper into a small pill bottle. Fill the bottle with pickling spice and replace the lid. Bury it where three roads meet, because such a spot is dedicated to Hecate, the goddess of sorcery.

To silence a rival

On a small piece of new, white paper, write in black ink the name of the person who is causing you grief. Draw a thick black square around the person's name. Put the piece of paper under an upturned glass and leave it there to restrict your love rival. The adversary may be able to see and hear you but will be unable to harm you or your love relationship because your spell will block the bad, divisive influence.

To stop a love opponent

Write the name of your love rival in black ink on a small, jagged piece of black paper. The name will barely be noticeable. Insert the piece of paper into a small glass pill bottle. Sprinkle in seven pinches of salt and put in seven pins. Fill the bottle with cold water and seal the contents with the lid. Bury the bottle so that the glass end is pointing in the compass direction of your rival's home.

To cool the pace of love

Light a blue candle. Take a passion fruit and a small bowl of crushed ice or ice cubes, and at midnight, place the passion fruit in the bowl. Sit with the candle until the ice melts to water. Give the passion fruit to your lover to eat, or eat the fruit yourself.

To end bitterness

Light a white candle and cut a lemon in half beside it. Write the embittered person's name on a small piece of white paper. Place the piece of paper on top of one of the lemon halves and insert a pin through the name. Secure the two halves together with seven pins to make a whole lemon. Keep the lemon on a windowsill. The person's bitterness for you will subside. When the lemon dries, bury it.

To silence gossip

Write the gossiper's name in blue ink on a small square of purple paper. Place the piece of paper into a small, empty bottle, then fill the bottle with garlic cloves or powder. Bury the bottle outside or in an indoor pot to stifle the gossiper's words.

Three crows flying together is a marriage sign.

To break the bonds
of a love triangle

At eleven o'clock on a Friday night, light three candles and place them in a triangle shape—one red for the one you love, one pink for you, and one blue for your love rival. At midnight snuff out the blue candle while saying: *"Your love is extinguished."* Move the red and pink candles side by side. Sit with the candles while they burn for a while, then snuff them out. ¶ If possible, bury the blue candle the following day where three roads meet to form a fork shape. On consecutive nights relight the red and pink candles side by side until both candles are exhausted and burn out naturally in your presence. Bury the remaining wax from both candles in a small hole in the ground, in a garden, or in an indoor pot.

May morning
willow divination

Willow is an emblem of grief and unrequited love, but it can also ease a broken heart. On a May morning write the name of your lost lover in blue ink on pink paper. Place the paper under a vase of willow. If you do not hear from your heartbreaker before the willow fades, it is a sign that your lover will not return. Bury the willow and paper to lay the relationship to rest and exorcise haunting memories.

To blow his/her feelings away

Light a white candle. Write his or her name on a piece of paper. Burn the paper in the flame and leave it to extinguish in a saucer. Take the saucer outside and blow the ash into the breeze.

To ease a broken heart

Onions are ruled by the planet Mars and are said to resemble the cosmos. The core is the earth and the heart is the moon. The layers outside the heart are the seven spheres of the seven planets. Angels guard each sphere. The outside skin represents God, to which fixed orbits cling. ¶ Light a blue candle. Take an onion and gently peel away each layer. Place the layers in a saucer in front of the candle. Emotions make spells work, and if the onion makes you cry, it is purging you from pent-up emotions and will clear the air. After an hour snuff out the candle. Boil the onion skins until the water turns yellow, then throw both the water and skins away, or bury the onion pieces outdoors, where the earth will quickly diminish negativity.

[109]

When someone you don't like
    is making romantic overtures,
blow across your fingertips
    to distance this person from you.

To stop dreaming
of a lover

The morning after dreaming of a lover you wish you had never met or wish to be free from, give your bedroom a spring cleaning. Open your windows wide, strip the bed, and change the sheets. Vacuum underneath and around all sides of your bed, including the mattress, and if you store things under your bed, remove the items and keep them elsewhere. Close the windows when the sun is going down, or earlier if you are leaving your home to go out. ¶ At nighttime, concoct a peace potion: five drops of lavender oil, five drops of rose oil, and ten drops of almond oil. Light a white candle in the bathroom and take a bath or shower. Gaze into the flame while washing. It represents the eternal power of light over darkness and good over evil. Lavender, governed by the planet Mercury, rules communication, and rose, ruled by the planet Venus, attracts love. ¶ While washing or relaxing, dab your forefinger into the peace potion to anoint your head, neck, wrists, and heels with the oil. When you remove the plug from the bath or as you shower, consciously think that your former lover's negative influence on you is being washed away. ¶ After bathing, get ready for bed. Carry the candle and peace potion to your bedroom and place the candle in front of your dressing-table mirror. Anoint the four corners of your bed and the center of your pillow with the peace potion. The four corners of the bed represent earth, air, fire, and water, and where you lay your head on your pillow represents you. Anoint your forehead with the remaining oil, snuff out the candle, and have sweet dreams. The love that haunts you will stop pervading your sleep.

To end a relationship

Light a white candle. In blue ink on white paper, write the name of the person you wish to release. Open an atlas or dictionary and place the piece of paper on a page. Ring a bell, quickly close the book, and immediately snuff out the candle. After fourteen days, remove the piece of paper and bury it.

[111]

To heal love's hurt

Using a needle and red string, thread thirteen garlic cloves. Tie the ends of the string to form a circular shape. Bury the garlic or toss it into a stream, pond, river, or the sea for your pain to be washed away with the flow of the current.

In blue ink on white paper, write the name of the one who has broken your heart. Sprinkle sage onto the paper to absorb negativity. Wrap the paper to seal the sage and bury both. As the sage and paper disintegrate, the pain in your heart will fade.

To end bitterness

To turn a bitter heart sweet, write the embittered person's name in fountain-pen ink on a small, heart-shaped piece of clean, white paper. Light a white candle and place it beside a saucer. Drop the piece of paper into the saucer and pour vinegar over it until it is soaked. The vinegar will dissolve the ink and any bitterness, adding and inducing color into the life of the person you named. ¶ After half an hour, drain the vinegar from the paper. Ink lifted from the paper will cleanse the person's aura, and the writing will appear much more legible again. ¶ Let the paper dry. On the following day, burn it at midnight by holding it to the flame of a new blue candle. Drop the paper into a dish to extinguish.

Now that it's over

Using a pin, inscribe a white candle with your name. On blue paper in blue ink, write the name of the one you wish to depart from. Place the paper on a saucer and pour melted wax over the person's name. Pierce the name with a pin and bury the pin and paper outdoors with three garlic cloves to exorcise him or her from your life. Alternately, use an indoor pot of soil and throw the soil containing the paper away after a few days. Allow the candle to burn down past the inscription before snuffing it out.

Finding a shell means you will

To clear the air from haunting memories

When unhappy dreams and memories haunt your sleep, cast a spell on the night of a full moon, using a concoction of full moon jinx removing oil: five drops of camphor oil and five drops of peppermint oil. ¶ At five minutes to midnight, anoint a candle with the full moon jinx removing oil. Rub the oil with your fingertips down from the candle's wick (representing the North Pole) to the center, and up from the base (representing the South Pole) to the center. ¶ Turn off any lights in the room and light the candle at midnight while saying: *"I am free from those who wish to harm my mind, body, or soul."* The flame may flicker quite wildly, so sit with the candle while it burns. At one o'clock in the morning, snuff out the candle.

[113]

To free your heart

Light a yellow or orange candle on a Sunday night. Ignite and burn a few strands of your former lover's hair or threads of fabric from his or her clothes while saying: *"My heart is healed, my mind is free. Love's victim I will no longer be."* Snuff out the candle. Repeat the spell for six more nights if possible.

hear from the one you love.

To reverse a spell

The origin of the universe comes from good. A curse is not harmonious to the love force, and if you cast one, it will work against and return to you. There are ways, however, to reverse spells that you have cast. There is an old and very true saying: *"Be careful what you wish for; it may come true."* Wishes do come true because emotions make spells work. You may have a change of heart after you work your magic. What you wished for then may not be what you wish for now. There are antidotes to rectify spells that have made wishes come true. ¶ If when your wish is granted by a spell you change your mind, write on white paper: *"I wish the spell I have cast for [name of person] to be washed away."* Dissolve the spell by dropping the white paper into a bowl of clean water. Pour the water away. ¶ Light a white candle. Write your name and the name of the one you have spellbound on a clean piece of white paper and burn the paper in the flame. Place the paper in a saucer to extinguish to ash. Snuff out the candle. Blow the ash away in the wind. ¶ Write backward from right to left the spell you wish to reverse. Crumple the piece of paper and place it in a small dish of soil to keep indoors for nine days. After the nine days, throw the soil away. ¶ Write the name of the person you have spellbound on a new piece of white paper. Light a white candle. Burn the paper in the flame and place it in a dish until it has completely reduced to ash. Snuff out the candle. Blow

[114]

the ash away into the wind or empty it from a window. ¶ Place earth in a flowerpot, insert a white candle into the soil, and light the wick. After fifteen minutes remove the candle and place it upside down in the soil to extinguish the flame. Trim the wax at the base of the candle to expose the wick, and light the reverse candle end to reverse your spell. After fifteen minutes snuff the candle out and bury it outdoors.

Once it is over

Take a piece of wood to represent your ex-partner. Toss the wood onto a bonfire and watch it burn. The rising smoke represents the dissipating spirit of the relationship. The remaining ash represents the dead relationship.

[115]

To separate

Light two candles side by side, one to represent you and the other to signify the person you wish to detach from. Once the flames are established, move the candles to increase the divide. Look at the flame while saying: "[*Name of person*], *leave my heart. I banish you. Depart!*" At intervals between gazing into the flame and separating the candles, repeat the words until finally the candles are distanced as far away from each other as possible. Snuff out both candles, or burn them in an indoor fireplace or on a bonfire; then bury them.

To rid an ex-lover
from your mind

On the night of a full moon and for thirteen consecutive nights, light a blue candle. Write the name of the one you wish to break free from in chalk on white paper. Tear the paper into tiny pieces and flush them away. ¶ On the fourteenth night, burn the piece of paper and leave it to extinguish in a bowl with high sides. Take the ash outside and throw it over your left shoulder and far away. Walk indoors without looking over your shoulder or turning around. If the ash falls or is blown onto your clothes, it is a sign that your former lover will not easily let you go. If this happens, write his or her name again, burn it in the flame, leave the paper to reduce to ash, and add seven pinches of salt to the ash before returning outside to cast the mixture over your left shoulder, without looking back. Salt is a symbol of the pure soul.

It is said to bring you a lucky response if you kiss an important letter when you pop it into the mailbox.

Good luck in
LOVE

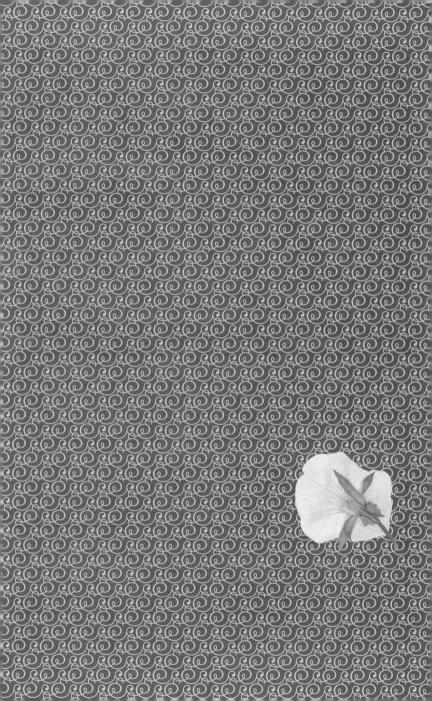

You can attract good luck in love, but you can also read natural signs that speak the language of love. Your soul possesses powers of omniscience, the ability to know everything. An inquisitive mind stirs your psyche while guiding you to truth.

Venus lucky love sachet

Take a red handkerchief. Using a pin or a pen, write your own name and the name of the one you love on a bay leaf. Ruled by the sun, bay will instill sunshine into love. ¶ Place the bay leaf on top of the center of the handkerchief. Sprinkle in sage, thyme, rose petals, daisies, two dried beans, and two hazelnuts, because all are ruled by the love planet, Venus. Using a red ribbon, tie the handkerchief around the ingredients—scooped into a ball shape—so that the outer edges of the handkerchief are pointing upward and outward. Sleep with the Venus sachet under your pillow or keep it close to you.

[119]

Light a white candle at five to twelve. At midnight say:
"The bonds of love be broken, while these few words are spoken."
Snuff out the candle.

Love Pouch

To attract and meet a true love, tie a sprig of rosemary in a handkerchief. If you have someone particular in mind, choose the ribbon color that matches the person's astrological birth sign. Otherwise, use a ribbon or cord that represents your own astrological color:

- ARIES & SCORPIO: *red*
- TAURUS & LIBRA: *green*
- GEMINI AND VIRGO: *purple or lilac*
- CANCER: *white*
- LEO: *yellow*
- SAGITTARIUS & PISCES: *blue*
- CAPRICORN AND AQUARIUS: *black*

[120]

The key to the treasure of your name

Names are unique, and your moniker is your own personal talisman. You can divine magic with it. Asking your inner voice to inspire a name for a baby or pet may have more to it than you realize. Using the letters of your first and last names to form words may lead to a small or large discovery. In some cases no words can be formulated. The words that are found express part of your psyche and personality. ¶ You can also make an anagram from the first and last names of the one you love. Words that are found are part of your lover's nature. If you make an anagram from both your name and your sweetheart's name combined, the words you are able to formulate reveal your fate with the person.

Name amulet

To make your name a magical lucky charm to carry or keep, join the letters that spell words and discard any superfluous letters. Write your name in cursive writing on green paper in gold ink. Write the word or words made from the anagram of your name in a circular shape and sign the paper in gold ink. Keep the paper as an amulet. ¶ To influence love for a season or a year of your life, write the words derived from your name in gold ink on pink paper in a circular shape. The last letter should join the first as a sign of an eternal circle. That circle will protect you. When words cannot be formulated from letters in your full name, write your name in cursive writing using gold ink on a piece of green paper in a circular shape. Sign the piece of paper in gold ink and keep the amulet close to you. ¶ To bind a lover to you, sign your name in a semicircular shape in gold ink on red paper. Join your name with your lover's name so that both names form a circular shape. By binding your lover's name to yours, you will share in your suitor's destiny until you burn or bury the talisman with love.

A love bond

When you and your lover are walking in nature, both of you should form each other's names in leaves placed on the ground. Holding hands, walk three times in a clockwise circle around the names and then run away together as fast as you can.

Psychic bath salts

Alone or with friends, thoroughly mix three table-spoons of Epsom salts, two tablespoons of baking powder, and one tablespoon of ground rock or sea salt. Add a handful of fresh or dried lavender flowers. Add two drops of myrrh, one drop of frankincense, and two drops of sandalwood. Stir with a spoon and then mix with your fingers. The ingredients, enough for three treatments, will increase your psychic powers when added to your bathwater.

Love luck divinations

While tossing a salad with dressing, count the number of lettuce leaves that fall from the bowl. Each leaf designates one year before marriage. ¶ Place one broad bean in a dish of peas. The person who finds the bean on his or her plate when the peas are served is said to be the next to marry.

Place two acorns side by side on a windowsill to encourage

Friendly wishes

Alone or with one or more friends, spin around three times in a clockwise circle while thinking your personal wishes and saying: *"To begin this wish I spin, when spun my wish is begun."* More than one wish is allowed, but each wish requires three spins and one verse.

Secret wishes

Light a blue candle. In front of the candle, write your wish in milk with a paintbrush on a small piece of white paper. After a few minutes, hold the piece of paper about an inch away from the flame. When the heat of the fire turns the invisible writing golden brown, your wish will begin to come true.

Best wishes

You and your lover should each write your wishes using milk and paintbrushes on small pieces of clean, white paper. Swap the wishes with each other. When you are alone and your partner is also alone, hold the piece of paper to the heat of a white candle flame. The written wishes will appear in golden brown writing. When the wish has been read, burn the paper in the flame and allow it to extinguish to ash in a dish.

the one you love to feel so strongly for you that he or she visits your home.

Katie Boyle's French recipe for a happy life together

This recipe was given to me by British TV personality Katie Boyle. The recipe was given to Katie by her step-mother, Lady Becker, whose marriage to Katie's father was happy despite her being thirty-two years older than her husband, the Marchese Demetrio. Lady Becker was sixty-two and Demetrio thirty when they wed.

> *To begin with, put into a bowl,*
> *Two or three pounds of hope.*
> *Then you add a ton of caring and understanding.*
> *Now comes a measure of kindness and*
> *A hundred weight of trust.*
> *Put in what you will of gaiety,*
> *And four or five pots of obedience,*
> *To blend with five or six pounds of sweetness.*
> *There's no need whatsoever for monotony,*
> *And be sure you add to good humor.*
> *Just a dash of madness.*
> *As for salt, not more than one grain*
> *Because if you have more of this,*
> *Instead of one ounce,*
> *You'll have to put at least two of patience.*
> *Now simmer the mixture at a well-sustained heat,*
> *And never lose sight of either love or friendship.*
> *By doing all this you will have cooked a well-balanced pie,*
> *A slice of which each morning,*
> *Will be enough to embellish your life.*

Conclusion

When casting love spells, you may be amazed to see your heartfelt wishes magically come true and miraculously fulfill your heart's desires. Your emotions and faith are strong spell ingredients that are also powerful when weaving love magic for others. May your own life and the lives of those you care about never be without love.

[127]

A deep red rose blooming
in your garden before June
foretells a family wedding.

FIRST EDITION

Book design by Julia Sedykh Design

Library of Congress Cataloging-in-Publication Data
Kemp, Gillian
The love magic book : potions for passion and
recipes for romance / by Gillian Kemp.
p.cm.
ISBN 0-316-39947-7
I. Magic. 2. Love — Miscellanea. I. Title.

BF1623.L6 K46 2003
133.4'42 — dc21   2002069451

10 9 8 7 6 5 4 3 2 1

LAKE

Printed in the United States of America

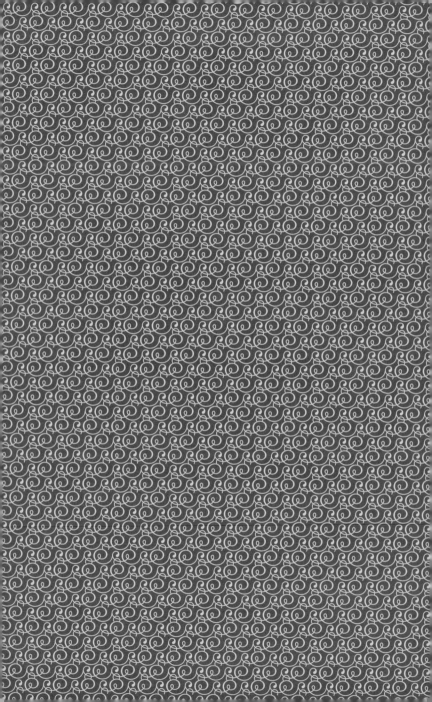